Sprinkles of Dreams

Let your dreams sprinkle happiness

Ayushi Arora

ISBN 978-93-5610-392-4
© Ayushi Arora 2022
Published in India 2022 by Pencil

A brand of

One Point Six Technologies Pvt. Ltd.
123, Building J2, Shram Seva Premises,
Wadala Truck Terminal, Wadala (E)
Mumbai 400037, Maharashtra, INDIA
E connect@thepencilapp.com
W www.thepencilapp.com

10
Unidades.

SPRINKLES OF DREAMS

AYUSHI ARORA

Author biography

With the mindset of "Let your dreams sprinkle happiness," Ayushi Arora started writing this book when she was in her freshman year i.e., 9th grade. Ayushi is a young poet and an aspiring singer born and brought up in Delhi. She is currently pursuing Journalism and Mass Communication from JIMS VK, Delhi. She started writing short poems and verses at the age of 9. Later, as she grew up, she developed an interest in music and started writing songs of her own. As a person who writes about fiction and fantasy, she always wanted her work to be published and for others to relate to what she wrote. After thinking for years and developing the courage to share her work with the world, she collected the poems that she wrote over the years and transformed them into "Sprinkles of Dreams". For another one of her dreams, singing, Ayushi has her Instagram page with the name @teddy.sings that is solely focused on her music. She is also a huge believer in the quote "Treat People With Kindness".

CONTENTS

Nature's Immortality

The winds that blow
My mind from the dark
The waves that drown
My loneliness by a spark

The tides that pull me
From the depth of immortality
The moon that shines
My world so magically

When I sit by the ocean
My life feels like heaven
When I hear the birds babbling
My life turns into a blessing

I used to wonder if this beauty
Will last in the future
But, now I realize
This is the immortality of nature

A Dream

I look around and all I see
Is just you and me
And then, I woke up to realize
It was all just a dream

I really can't explain how
You mean the world me
The way I feel for you
and the way you loved me
But maybe it was all just a dream
Yeah now I know it was all just a dream

Its been so long since I saw
You smile because of me
Honey, I can't tell how much I miss
When we were together
In a land of fantasy
But now I know it was all just a dream
Yeah now I know it was all just a dream

The way I feel for you
and the way you loved me
And baby now I know how much
We were meant to me
But maybe it will all be a dream
Yeah now I know it was all just a dream

Quote 1

"I believed in magic, just for a fraction of a second."

- Ayushi Arora

A New Beginning

The end of an era
The start of something new
It's a whole new era
So let your dreams be pursued!

Write your own story
With twists and turn
Sparkled with the glory
Let the negative bridges burn

Climb the mountain of fantasy
For there is nothing holding you down
Reach the high level of ecstasy
And build your own dream town

Time waits for none
Let your dreams be released
Take a chance to be number one
God knows you've tried atleast

Ups and downs, Fake jewels and crowns
Whatever comes your way
Don't ever hold your head down
Cause it will be over by the end of the day

Be yourself, believe in you
Happiness is surely coming your way!

Imaginary City

It was a place of imagination
The place of my dreams
Maybe my own creation

A place with beaches and mountains and trees
A place where I felt like home
A place where there was no one to tease

On the beaches having fun with the waves
I could swim and run and play
Yes, I want those days

I would sing my favorite song
And do whatever I want
I would ask my friends to come along

It was a place of imagination
The place of my dreams
Yes, it was my own creation

I wish, soon come that days
This dream no longer should stay a dream
Sitting on the beach with the sun rays

Quote 2

Mend all your scars with desire and they will surely heal.

- Ayushi Arora

More Than This

Days have passed
And I am still here
My loneliness
Is becoming my fear
But baby I won't ever stop
Cause my heart belongs with you

And I wish that
Maybe one day
You'll make me feel
That we can be something
More than this

And I wish that
Then we will be
What I have ever wished
Cause we can be something
More than this

Darling, all I want is you
Why can't you realise that too

That your the one made for me
Don't you see
What we could be

And I wish that
Maybe one day
You'll fall for me
And then we'll be something
More than this

And I know that
Then we won't be
We won't be lonely
Cause we would be something
More than this

Cursed Love

That Sunday morning

The blooming rose shined

With the air of love in the garden

She fell for the thorn

They breathed the same air

Stole each others hearts

Filled the whole garden with love

And became each other's best parts

All the flowers envied this unique bond

Tried to curse them down

But the love the thorn had

Kept the rose safe and sound

All their fights with their friends

It was all in vain

One cursed day

With the storm around the corner

The rose with all her petals flowing away

Tried to hold onto her love, the thorn

Little did they know

The curse from the other flowers had worked

With the thorns' sharpness seeping through roses heart

She got killed by her love that night.

Quote 3

"Not all scars are meant to stay forever."

- Ayushi Arora

War zone

A sudden thought
Has just struck my mind
Why does this always happen
All of a sudden this whole world
Changes itself into a place undefined
All of us start fighting and loving
Just after a short gap
And if something miserable happens
Our life gets twisted like an Eminem rap
Even though we care and then we fight
We will never forget that
We cannot take away anything
That God gave us as our birthright
It's strange to see that
This beautiful world suddenly changes itself into a war
zone
But one day we will be fully grown
To know the harms of a war
Then the policy of war will be thrown
And this world will no longer be known
As a war zone...

PEACE ??

Don't

Don't cry
Don't show anyone
how weak you are
Show the world what you can be
Don't let anyone get to you
Make them realise what you are
Don't let anyone break you

Don't cry
Don't show anyone
How weak you are
Let them know that you can be brave
Let them know what they are messing with
Never trust someone so much
That it breaks you
When they leave
Don't let anyone play with your heart

Don't cry
Don't show the world
How weak you are
No one is worth your tears my love

Live your life in your own style
No one can stop you to do so
Don't be anyone's puppet

Don't cry
Don't show the world
How weak you are

Quote 4

"We are all tied in the same loop with no way to escape."

- Ayushi Arora

Together

You are my life
Without you, there is nothing to survive
I just wanna fall deep into your eyes
But without you, there is no sunrise

I am a body
You are a soul
I want to die in your arms
When I fall

When I think about you
I am on cloud nine
You are the one who
Brings me my sunshine
You are an angel
Who took me to heaven
With you I feel magical 24/7

Together we are so strong
That no one can break our bond
Together we are so sweet
Nothing can stop us to meet

I can't imagine
My life without you
Lovers like us are only a few
Love like you is hard to find
With your love
I'm completely blind

Anxiety

This rollercoaster
I'm riding
It's only going down and down

And I can
Feel my heartbreak
I can't seem to break free

These voices
In my head say
I don't deserve it

So come on and save me
From this nightmare or my
Worst Dream

Anxiety, Anxiety
Anxiety, anxiety
Suffocates me

This feeling
I'm feeling
I don't want to feel it

Can you hear me?
Can you leave me?

I wanna wake up
In a new world
Where I can be ME

So can you pull me?
Be my anchor?
Cause I've reached rock bottom

So come on and wake me
From this nightmare or my
Worst Dream

Anxiety, Anxiety

Anxiety, Anxiety

Suffocates me

This feeling
I'm feeling
I don't want to feel it
Can you hear me?
Can you leave me?

Now,
I've left you behind
No, I won't let you overpower my mind

Now,
I've left you behind
No, I won't let you overpower my mind

Anxiety, Anxiety
Anxiety, Anxiety
You don't own me

This feeling
I'm feeling
I feel like I like it
It's my destiny
No more anxiety
No more anxiety

Now,
I've left you behind
No, I won't let you overpower my mind

Quote 5

"The fake is getting faker up until there is nothing real left."

- Ayushi Arora

Give Me Wings To Fly

They've left me stranded
In the depth of darkness
Hear me cry out loud
But there is no one around

I won't be silenced
I will rise again
Just wait and you will see me
Flying high in the sky again

No one can tear my faith apart
I dare you, challenge me
Every danger, every fear
It will all lie beneath me

Give me wings to fly
and you won't see me come down
Give me wings to fly
And I will show you who is the queen.

Life

The most important thing
Which can help to survive
Jolliness and Happiness it brings
Our life is to live...

Everyone makes mistakes
it is our responsibility to forgive
Because life does not have any breaks
And alas, our life is to live...

How difficult it is to make decisions
About us and our life
And with many reasons
It is important to live
Our life is to live

Quote 6

"I'm losing the battle inside my mind."

- Ayushi Arora